WITHDRAWN

The Story of
Nintendo

Adam Sutherland

rosen publishing's
rosen central

New York

Nintendo Rules the World!

Nintendo is a phenomenally successful company that leads the world in the creation of video games. It has made a global business out of having fun.

According to its company Web site, Nintendo Co., Ltd., based in Kyoto, Japan, manufactures and markets hardware and software for its Wii and DS systems. Since 1983, when it launched the Nintendo Entertainment System (NES), the company has sold 4 billion video games, creating household names of characters like Mario, Donkey Kong, Zelda, and Pokémon. It has also sold more than 565 million consoles around the world, including the current-generation Wii, Nintendo DS, DSi, and DSi XL, as well as the Game Boy, Game Boy Advance, Super NES, Nintendo 64, and Nintendo GameCube.

Valued at $85 billion, Nintendo is the third largest company in Japan. It is so strong that not only was it able to withstand 2008's global recession virtually unaffected, it actually helped keep the whole video game industry afloat. While around the world companies' profits were falling through the floor, according to US research firm NPD, in January 2009 the US video game market (hardware and software) had actually grown 13 percent relative to the previous year. Most of that growth was thanks to Nintendo products. The hardware leader was the Wii, at 680,000 units, followed by the DS at 510,000. The top three software titles were all Wii games, with Wii Fit selling 780,000 copies, breaking the record for January sales.

Company President Iwata in front of two of ➤ Nintendo's best-loved inventions — Mario and Yoshi.

From simple beginnings, Nintendo has developed a reputation for innovation that puts it on a par with fellow global brands like Apple and Google. Over the following pages we will explore the secret of Nintendo's success, looking at the company's origins, its corporate philosophy, its most memorable products, the different departments in Nintendo, and the people who continue to make it successful. Are you ready to play?

▲ *A young fan gazes at Nintendo's GameCube at its launch at the Nintendo Space World exhibition in 2000.*

> **❝** What kind of a company is Nintendo? We're a manufacturer of smiles. That's what any entertainment company should be... It's fun for us when we see people's reactions, and it's what lets us keep doing our job. **❞**
>
> **Company President Satoru Iwata**

CHAPTER 2
Seizing the Opportunity

Nintendo Koppai was founded in the Japanese city of Kyoto by a wood-block printer, Fusajiro Yamauchi, in 1889. The company made "hanafuda" and "karuta" playing cards — originally from the bark of mulberry trees!

Fusajiro's young company (loosely translated, Nintendo means "leave luck to the stars") enjoyed a boom in sales that resulted when both types of cards were legalized by the Japanese government. However, by 1902 the government imposed a high tax on the cards to help fund its war efforts in China and Russia, and many card manufacturers went out of business.

So how did Nintendo survive when others failed? Fusajiro was an intelligent and daring entrepreneur who provided what customers wanted and stayed one

Business Matters

Diversification — Companies often decide to offer new products or services because it reduces the risk of its other products becoming too limited or uninteresting. Nintendo moved from playing cards into children's games and the electronics market. By adding new products to its range, Nintendo is protecting its sales figures. When one section of its market "underperforms," or sells less than expected, the others can compensate.

Young Japanese women playing cards in traditional dress.

step ahead of the competition. For example, Nintendo was the first Japanese company to see a gap in the market for producing Western-style (i.e. paper) playing cards, which had previously only been available in Japan as costly imports.

Fusajiro was also a great networker. He realized that playing cards and cigarettes were being bought by the same groups of people — gamblers! So he struck up a friendship with another Kyoto-based businessman, Kichibei Murai, who was the first person to manufacture and sell paper-rolled cigarettes in Japan. Fusajiro used his friend's nationwide distribution network to sell his playing cards around Japan, and, by 1926, Nintendo was the largest card company in the country.

In the same year, Fusajiro's son-in-law, Sekiryo, took over the company and renamed it Yamauchi Nintendo. Nintendo continued to manufacture playing cards through the 1950s. However, a turning point for the company came when Fusajiro's grandson, Hiroshi, visited the United States Playing Card Company. Although they were by far the biggest card manufacturer in America, Hiroshi was surprised by how small their offices were. By this time, the company had been renamed Nintendo Playing Card Company, but this visit made Hiroshi realize that the playing card business had its limits, and that he would need to investigate other areas that would help Nintendo keep growing.

Brains Behind the Brand

Fusajiro Yamauchi — founder of Nintendo

The founder of a company is often an entrepreneur — someone who sees an opportunity in the market and starts a company to meet that opportunity. Fusajiro Yamauchi founded Nintendo Koppai on November 6, 1889, making "hanafuda" cards for a game that was very popular in Japan at the time. The cards were made of tree bark and hand-painted by Fusajiro in his shop. When demand started to exceed his ability to make the cards on his own, Fusajiro hired a small staff. In 1907, Nintendo began manufacturing Western-style cards and, over the next two decades, became Japan's largest manufacturer of playing cards. Fusajiro retired in 1929, passing control of the business to his son-in-law, Sekiryo Kaneda Yamauchi. Fusajiro died in 1940.

Hiroshi Yamauchi (left) and Konami President Kozuki in Tokyo in 1999. Konami produces and publishes games. Yamauchi and Kozuki started a joint venture to develop software for Nintendo's future game machines.

CHAPTER 3

From Playing Cards to Electronics

Fusajiro's grandson, Hiroshi Yamauchi, was responsible for creating the company we know today. He was with Nintendo for 52 years, and turned the company from a playing card manufacturer into a global video game giant.

Business Matters

Company investment —
Companies invest money in certain areas — for example, Research and Development — with the aim of making higher profits in the future. Company investment into Research and Development can lead to the creation of "intellectual capital". This might take the form of a new games console or a new game that will become a bestseller and increase the company's profits. Return on investment (ROI) is a key measure of a firm's performance.

Hiroshi Yamauchi was charismatic, and had great business instincts. He was not a gamer, or even an expert in electronics, but he remained focused on what the consumer wanted — from playing cards to electronic games.

After his visit to the USA in 1956, Yamauchi agreed to a license deal with Walt Disney to use well-known cartoon characters on his playing cards. The idea helped Nintendo open up a new market in children's games, and this success took Yamauchi down a new path. Nintendo would branch out and investigate new markets beyond playing cards. In 1963 the company changed its name to what it is known as today — Nintendo Co., Ltd.

A clever and ambitious businessman, Yamauchi was always looking for new areas to invest in. Between 1963 and 1968, Nintendo launched several new

Nintendo returned to its roots with the extremely popular Pokémon trading cards.

businesses, including a taxi company, a TV network, and a food company (selling Popeye noodles and Disney food seasonings). None of these areas proved to be the success that Yamauchi was hoping for, and all were eventually closed.

After the 1964 Tokyo Olympics, there was a further drop in sales, and Nintendo's stock price fell to its lowest recorded levels as people became less interested in playing cards. Yamauchi was convinced that cards were a thing of the past; he decided that games were the future! Nintendo's first launch in the Japanese toy market was the Ultra Hand, an extendable "robot" arm, made out of an early version of Meccano (a brand of erector sets) which went on sale in 1966. It was not an overnight success, but it showed Yamauchi that he was on the right path and convinced him to try new things.

A poster advertising the Tokyo Olympics.
Nintendo's share price fell as people
became more interested in sports and
less interested in cards.

CHAPTER 4

Building a Reputation for Fun

Under the influence of its first Head of Development, Gunpei Yokoi, Nintendo started to produce some of the world's first electronic games.

Yokoi left Nintendo in 1996 to set up his own toy company, Koto Co., but was killed in a car accident the following year.

In the mid-1960s, there was no computer electronics industry and certainly no computer games. In fact, electronics graduate Yokoi joined Nintendo in 1965 as a maintenance man for the company's playing card assembly line machinery.

By the following year, Yokoi's reputation for weird and wonderful inventions had reached company president Yamauchi. Yokoi had invented the Ultra Hand (see page 12) in his spare time, and Yamauchi was so impressed that he launched the product in time for Christmas 1966. By 1970, Ultra Hand had sold 1.2 million units in Japan, and Yokoi had been moved from maintenance to the new Nintendo Games department as a product developer.

In 1970 the company released another Yokoi breakthough — the Ray Gun SP, a child's gun that fired a "laser" at a target. A direct hit caused the target to light up and make sounds. This was Nintendo's first high-tech/low-tech product — it used a light bulb in the gun, and a photovoltaic cell (the same technology as in solar panels) in the target. It was simple, but ingenious — the same principles that Nintendo is still employing today.

Brains Behind the Brand

Gunpei Yokoi — Nintendo's first head of development
Yokoi's inventions helped turn Nintendo from a playing card company into a toy and games company. An electronics graduate, he invented Nintendo's first toy, the Ultra Hand, in 1970. He went on to create the Game & Watch series, the Game Boy, the Virtual Boy (the world's first 3D games system), and did extensive work on the system that became the Nintendo Entertainment System (NES).

" [Hiroshi Yamauchi] couldn't stand making the same kind of toy the other guy was making, so whatever you showed him, you knew he was going to ask, 'How is that different from what everyone else is doing?' The worst way to answer was to tell him, 'It's not different, it's just a little better.' He'd be furious. "

Nintendo President Iwata on his predecessor

Next, Yamauchi gave Yokoi the challenge of designing inexpensive handheld games. Yokoi and his Research and Development team began to experiment with cheap liquid crystal display (LCD) technology (the same technology used in calculators), creating a line of games called Game & Watch, credit card-sized video games with one game per console that people could play while commuting to work.

The series grew to 59 titles between 1980 and 1986, selling over 40 million units and making history as the world's first handheld computer game. As the consoles were too small to incorporate a joystick, Yokoi also invented the + shaped directional pad, which players could use to move in four directions: up, down, left, and right. Yamauchi quickly patented the technology, and it has been used on every Nintendo game system since! Game & Watch also provided Nintendo with the profits it would put towards developing new gaming opportunities.

The Nintendo Zelda game for the DS is a much-loved favorite. Nintendo continues to invest in Research and Development so that they can capture children's imaginations.

THE LEGEND OF
ZELDA
Phantom
Hourglass

Nintendo

The Game Boy Arrives!

Nintendo has a reputation for leading the world in the development of handheld games. The trend started with Game & Watch, and took off with the release of the Game Boy in 1989.

All of Nintendo's products are the result of years of development work. Back in 1979, the company created two separate teams, R&D1 and R&D2 (R&D stands for Research and Development), running side by side but working on different projects. While R&D1, led by new Nintendo recruit Masayuki Uemura, started work on the console that would become the NES (see page 21), Yokoi's R&D2 team started looking for the follow-up to Game & Watch.

What they came up with was the Game Boy. Basically a Game & Watch with interchangeable games, it had a black and white screen and was so durable that the prototype was demonstrated to Yamauchi by being thrown onto the floor several times to prove it would keep working!

Nintendo had worked hard to keep the price competitive. The Game Boy retailed for 2,000 yen (about $25) cheaper than the NES console — giving gaming fans a financial reason to choose a handheld game over a console.

The Game Boy's big competitor was the Sega Game Gear, which came with a color screen and could even be turned into a portable television. Over 20 years later, however, the Game Boy has proved to be far more successful. Why? The Game Boy was lower tech, but much more user-friendly.

Business Matters

Research and Development —
Otherwise known as R&D, this is a business activity aimed at discovering solutions to problems or creating new goods and knowledge. R&D may result in ownership of intellectual property such as "patents", legal ownership of new products and the technology that produced them. A technology company like Nintendo has over 800 registered patents for the technology it has created!

The Game Boy has sold 118 million units worldwide since it was first launched in Japan in 1989.

Children in Shanghai, China, play their Game Boys during a school lunch break in 1997.

Nintendo made far more and better quality games available for the Game Boy — from Tetris to the *Pokémon* series. What's more, the Game Boy ran for 35 hours on four AA batteries, while the Game Gear needed six AA batteries, and drained them in just 2–3 hours! It was a big as a lunch box and weighed just over 1 pound (0.5 kg).

Like any great product designer, Yokoi focused on what he thought users would find most useful in a handheld game. And he was right!

CHAPTER 6
The Battle for Your Living Room

While the Game Boy was proving to be the market leader in handheld games, Nintendo was fighting — and losing — a ten-year "war" with Sony over dominance of the home games console market.

Games fans expect great graphics, but they also expect games that are fun to play.

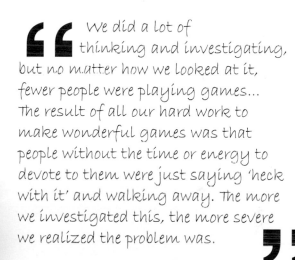

Nintendo invented the modern video game industry when it launched the NES (Nintendo Entertainment System) in 1983. But for a decade, from the mid-1990s onwards, Nintendo and Sony battled with each other to create ever-faster hardware and more spectacular graphics, dragging the evolution of games software behind them.

> " We did a lot of thinking and investigating, but no matter how we looked at it, fewer people were playing games... The result of all our hard work to make wonderful games was that people without the time or energy to devote to them were just saying 'heck with it' and walking away. The more we investigated this, the more severe we realized the problem was. "
>
> *Satoru Iwata*

Nintendo loses the ten-year "war" with Sony
(m = million)

Sony PlayStation	On sale Dec. 1994	Sold 124.9m	Software titles 4,400
Nintendo 64	On sale June 1996	Sold 32.93m	Software titles 210
Sony PlayStation 2	On sale Mar. 2000	Sold 132m	Software titles 4,550
Nintendo GameCube	On sale Sept. 2001	Sold 21.74m	Software titles 280

SCE — a Sony subsidiary — released the first PlayStation (PS) in 1994, followed by the PS2 in 2000. The two consoles completely dominated the market. To follow its success, Sony invested over 200 billion yen ($2.6 billion) into creating the PS3.

For Nintendo, creating faster, more sophisticated game consoles didn't automatically mean they would sell well. The Nintendo 64's processing power gave it graphics far superior to the PlayStation. However, it was so complicated to create code for it that independent games designers turned their backs on it and designed for the simpler PlayStation instead.

When the Nintendo 64 launched in 1996, just two games had been developed for it. Six months later, only two more had been added, and a full year and a half after launch, only 50 titles were available. At the same time, over 1,000 games were available for the PlayStation.

It was a tough lesson, but one that proved valuable. The most important thing was not processing power or stunning graphics, it was something that gaming companies call "end user experience" — the enjoyment that users get from playing the games. Fortunately, Nintendo's sales of the Game Boy console and its games helped see the company through its troubled times. And Nintendo learned its lesson well, going on to develop the DS and the Wii.

Despite its Blu-ray capability, Sony's PS3 was eclipsed in sales by the Nintendo Wii (see page 35).

CHAPTER 7
The Business of Games Creation

Great games are what drive console sales. Nintendo's largest division —
Nintendo Entertainment Analysis and Development (EAD) — is dedicated
to creating games that fans will love and that will sell millions of copies.

The violent Grand Theft Auto *series, by
Nintendo competitor Rockstar North,
represents the complete opposite
approach to gaming from Nintendo's
family- and youth-friendly products.*

The Pokémon characters were created for a video game but became a popular TV series.

EAD is the most famous of all Nintendo's internal development teams, housing at least 850 of the company's 3,000 employees. It was founded in 1989, when the R&D3 and R&D4 departments were combined and given the job of creating titles for the Super Famicom (SNES) console. By 2005, R&D1 and R&D2 had also been absorbed into EAD. It now runs at least five teams, of 20 to 30 employees each, side by side.

All departments are led by Nintendo's most famous developers, Shigeru Miyamoto and Takashi Tezuka, but are managed by individual

> On my business card, I'm a company president... But my mind's that of a game developer... And at heart, I am a gamer.
>
> **Satoru Iwata**

Brains Behind the Brand

Satoru Iwata — company president

Iwata became only Nintendo's fourth president when he succeeded Hiroshi Yamauchi in 2002. Born in 1959, Iwata got the computing bug at 15, when he was given a Hewlett-Packard HP-65, the world's first programmable calculator. Iwata studied computer science in college. He then became a programmer for a company called HAL, before joining Nintendo in 2000. He has overseen the most productive and profitable period of Nintendo's history, with the release of the GameCube, the Wii, and the DS all boosting company profits. He is regarded as one of the world's most successful company presidents.

department heads, with each Development Group, as they are known, working on their own specific range of titles.

Development Group 1 has created *Nintendogs* and the *Mario Kart* racing series; Development Group 2 makes Wii-branded games like *Wii Sports* and *Wii Play*; Group 3 looks after the Zelda series; Group 4 specializes in recoding existing games when new consoles come on the market; and Group 5 is mainly responsible for Mario titles.

Nintendo's game development is the most successful of all the gaming companies. Of the 20 best-selling games of all time, Nintendo holds the top 11 places. Bestsellers include *Wii Play* (27.38 million), *Wii Fit* (22.61 million), *New Super Mario Brothers* (24.13 million) and Pokémon *Diamond and Pearl* (17.39 million). The nearest competitor is *Grand Theft Auto: San Andreas* for Sony's PS2, which sold 17.33 million.

Since Satoru Iwata took over as Nintendo's president in 2002, he has encouraged certain outside software developers to also create new titles for Nintendo consoles. This is common in the games industry, with companies such as Activision (who created the Call of Duty and Tony Hawk titles) and Electronic Arts (who specialize in sports) creating a range of must-play games, often across all consoles.

Satoru Iwata unveils the new DSi handheld game player in 2008.

Expanding the Games Market

The success of the Game Boy supported Nintendo through ten years of poor console sales. Its replacement — the DS and, later, the DSi — did even better, creating millions of new gamers!

Games companies cannot afford to stand still. Even if a product is selling well, they are already working on the follow-up — the next big thing that will keep the public interested and buying. Innovation — the creation of new and unique products — is what every great company strives for.

The former President of Nintendo, Hiroshi Yamauchi, left his successor Satoru Iwata with one instruction — build a Game Boy with two

▼ *Games like* Brain Training *helped the DS to appeal to different sections of society.*

screens. Twin screens could have meant more complicated games that would only appeal to advanced players, but Iwata and his head of software development, Shigeru Miyamoto, decided to try something completely different. They made the DS so simple that your parents and even your grandparents could use it!

Nintendo could see from its research that the gap between gamers and non-gamers was widening. Complicated controls not only put off non-gamers, they actually made people dislike the idea of video games. So the DS was developed with one of the screens as a touch screen, which made controlling games very simple. It also helped Nintendo create a new generation of titles — like *Nintendogs* (where you train and care for a virtual dog) and *Dr. Kawashima's Brain Training* (that helps you "exercise" your brain with a series of mental tasks) — that related to ordinary people's lives.

Released in the US and Japan in December 2004, the DS recaptured people who had drifted away from video games. By March 2009, it had broken the 100 million sales mark — faster than

Business Matters

Public relations (PR) — is the practice of conveying messages to the public through the media on behalf of a client, with the intention of changing the public's actions by influencing their opinions, for example towards buying a specific console or game. PR professionals usually target specific sections of the public ("audiences"), since similar opinions tend to be shared by a group of people rather than an entire society.

any other game system in history. By September 2010, the DS in all its forms had sold a massive 136 million units.

▼ *Nintendogs was one of the DS's first best-selling games.*

Just as importantly, its games brought in both younger and older players, and widened the DS's appeal. Among DS users whose first game was *Brain Training*, 35 percent bought another game within 90 days, and 10 percent bought at least 11 games. Nintendo had tapped into valuable new generations of gamers! In its first full year of sales, the DS helped Nintendo more than double company profits from $183.7 million to $480.3 million.

> **"** We're always looking at ways to keep innovating in the industry; to make gameplay more fun and a little bit different. We felt the DS would be a unique way to do that. **"**
>
> **Beth Llewellyn, Nintendo US Director of PR**

Mario — a Superstar for 30 years!

Every games company wants to create an icon — a character that becomes familiar to gamers of all generations. Probably the most famous gaming character of all time is a short plumber with blue dungarees and a moustache. His name is Mario.

Mario was the brainchild of head Nintendo designer Shigeru Miyamoto (see box opposite). The company's US division had launched in 1980 with a major push on an arcade game called *Radar Scope*. The game was unsuccessful, and Miyamoto was given the job of developing a new game that could run in the existing *Radar Scope* cabinets. He decided to hijack a game that was in development at the time for Game & Watch — *Popeye*. It would have name recognition in the USA, which should help sales.

However, Nintendo ran into problems with US cartoon studio Hanna-Barbera over the licensing of Popeye and other characters' images. So Miyamoto turned Popeye into "the old man," Olive Oyl became Princess Peach, and Bluto became the game's namesake Donkey Kong. The story is that Mario got his name from Mario Segale, the bad-tempered landlord of Nintendo's US warehouse.

Finally launched in 1981, the game was simple but addictive — Mario had to climb through a building site, avoiding the barrels thrown at him by a giant gorilla. It defined everything that Nintendo as a company stands for: wacky, harmless, non-violent family entertainment. It may be mostly kids who complete the game and save the princess, but mom and dad can play along, too, and not be put off by the game's content.

Mario generates massive amounts of revenue. Not only does a successful character help sell games (*Super Mario Brothers* has sold 250 million copies and is the most successful game franchise in the world), but a homemade creation also boosts company profits, by avoiding the sort of licence fees to outside companies that are necessary for games like *Tony Hawk's Skateboarding* or *Tiger Woods PGA Tour*. Who would bet on Mario not being around for another 30 years?

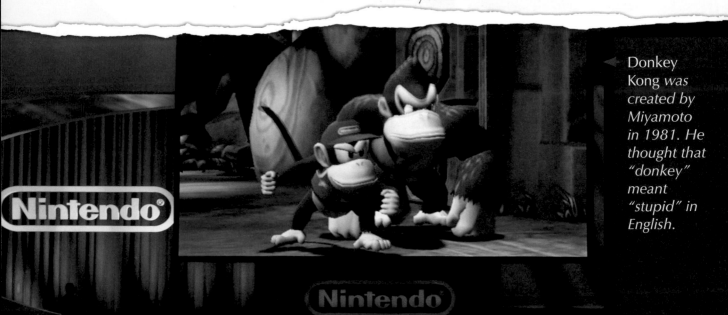

Donkey Kong *was created by Miyamoto in 1981. He thought that "donkey" meant "stupid" in English.*

Business Matters

Advertising — This is a form of communication intended to persuade an audience (viewers, readers, or listeners) to purchase or take some action regarding products, ideas, or services. Advertising includes the name of a product or service and how that product or service could benefit the consumer, in order to persuade the consumer to purchase that particular brand. These messages are viewed via various media, such as television, print, and the Web.

Brains Behind the Brand

Shigeru Miyamoto — chief of software development

Miyamoto is generally regarded as the greatest video game designer in the world. He has created some of the most successful games of all time, including *Mario*, *Donkey Kong*, and *The Legend of Zelda* (which was based on his own childhood experiences). Miyamoto loved cartoons, but studied industrial design in college before joining Nintendo in 1977. He worked with Gunpei Yokoi (see pages 14–15) designing the company's first coin-operated arcade game. He now oversees Nintendo's Entertainment Analysis and Development division (EAD).

▼ *Miyamoto has been named number one in* Time *magazine's 100 Most Influential People in 2007.*

▼ *Mario and his twin brother, Luigi.*

CHAPTER 10
Games the Whole Family Can Play

When Nintendo developed the Wii, it went against every piece of industry wisdom up to that point. The result was a less advanced console that the whole family wanted to play.

For years, home video game systems made use of new technology breakthroughs and created faster, more advanced consoles. Genyo Takeda, Nintendo's head of integrated research, was the man responsible for the development of every home game system from the NES to the GameCube. Coming five years after the GameCube, it was expected that the Wii would include five years' worth of advances in technology. This time, however, Iwata ordered Takeda not to create a super-powerful cutting edge system, but to find something "that mom has to like"!

The Wii's design was far more living room-friendly. Significant programming advances made it smaller and more compact than its competitors, using less electricity and avoiding the need for a noisy fan to cool down its components.

> Video games drive mom crazy... They're a nuisance as far as she's concerned. We realized that if we wanted to grow the gaming population, we had to build a console that no one in the family hated.
>
> **Genyo Takeda**

The Wii's motion sensor allows people to experience the fun of ten-pin bowling or tennis and created a whole new gaming experience.

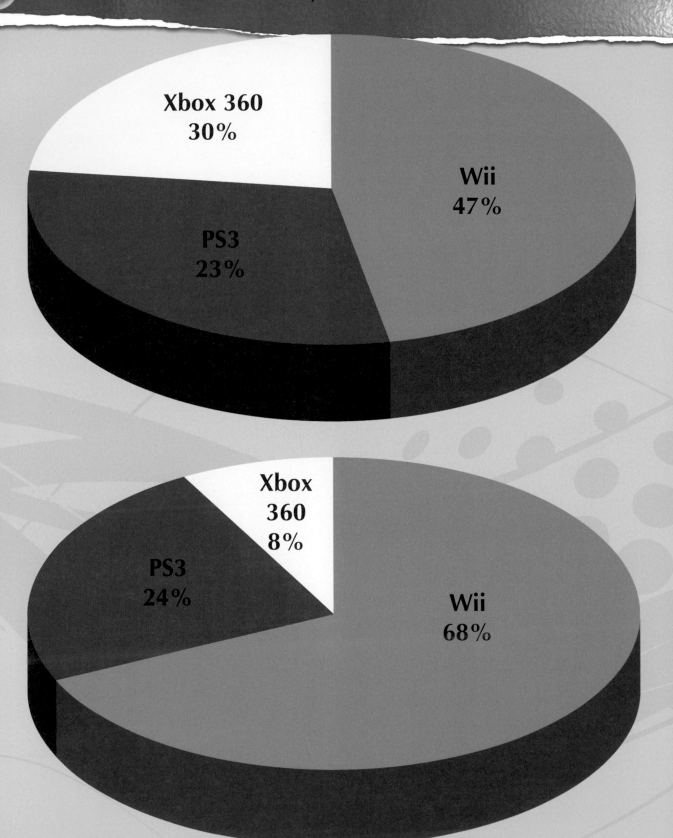

←

The Wii's percentage of sales in the global market.

What really made the Wii successful, though, was the new sensor technology of the controls that put players "into" the game, allowing them to physically "play" everything from ten-pin bowling to golf. The wireless controls, which use a light sensor and a sophisticated "accelerometer" to measure direction and speed, are fun and easy to use and were meant to attract large numbers of people who previously had no interest in playing video games.

The strategy worked. Although most industry experts forecast the Sony PlayStation 3, with its Blu-Ray player and amazing graphics, to be the big seller, it was actually the Wii that took the market by storm. Released in December 2006, it took just one year and eight months to break the 30 million sales barrier, smashing the PS2's record of two years and two months. By December 2008, the Wii had sold 44.96 million units worldwide — one-and-a-half times as many as the Xbox 360, and twice as many as the PS3. For the Wii, less was most definitely more!

←

The Wii's percentage of sales in the Japanese market.

CHAPTER 11

Games for Everyday Life

The Wii and the DS have attracted millions of new users to the games market. Now Nintendo is working hard to keep them there.

It's hard to survive these days without a computer or a mobile phone. But you don't need a video game console to live. So Nintendo is doing everything it can to make its consoles and games indispensable to everyday life.

Once the DS reached 20 million sales in Japan, it opened up the possibility of creating new services that millions of people could use. In May 2008, Nintendo Spot access points were installed at 21 locations in Tokyo. DS owners could use the wireless network to access news clips, weather forecasts, sports and entertainment news — turning their consoles from a simple gaming device into an information provider!

DS games like *Brain Training* and *Art Academy* have shown that game systems can be useful for training and education, and, with *Wii Sports* and *Wii Fit*, Nintendo has proven that games can also be good for your health! In the US, hotels

▼ *People trying out new games at the Tokyo Game Show in 2007.*

are installing Wii units as fitness equipment, and physiotherapy units in hospitals are using *Wii Fit* and *Wii Sports* to help rehabilitate patients after surgery or injury.

The Wii remote is also being used more and more as an actual TV remote, as Nintendo has developed a range of services that can be accessed through the Wii channel on a television. The Television Friend Channel provides eight days' worth of program information in 3D. Users can mark their favorite shows and have text messages sent to them when broadcast time is approaching.

The Wii Photo Channel can take all your favorite photos and turn them into an eye-catching slideshow.

President Iwata's continuing goal is to broaden Nintendo's business more and more into everyday life, creating new reasons for people to buy and use consoles that have nothing to do with gaming.

> " I think [Nintendo] has a lot in common with [Apple] in that we both make unique, interesting products that surprise people. I really respect and think highly of Nintendo. I myself own a GameCube and a Wii. "
>
> **Phil Schiller, senior vice president of Apple**

Business Matters

Retail sales — A retailer is a business that sells goods to the consumer, as opposed to a wholesaler or supplier, which normally sell goods to another business. Retailers include large businesses such as Nintendo, and also smaller, non-chain businesses run independently, such as a family-run bakery or bookshop.

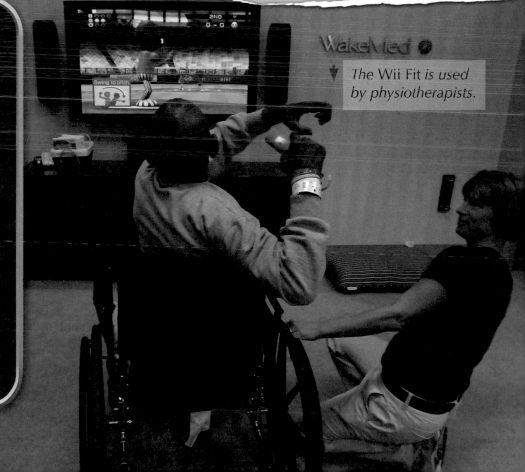

The Wii Fit is used by physiotherapists.

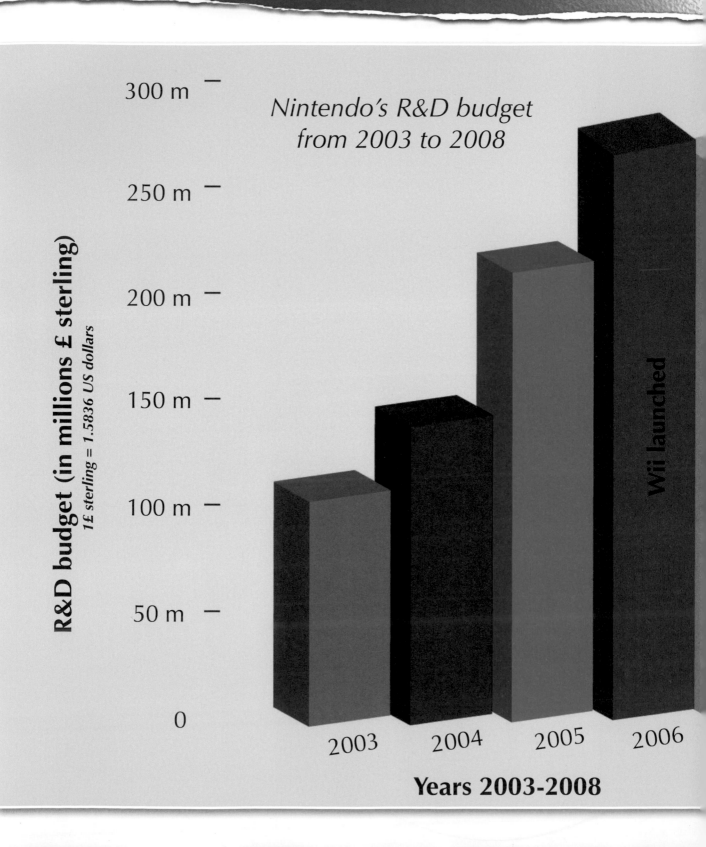

Nintendo's R&D budget from 2003 to 2008

R&D budget (in millions £ sterling)
1£ sterling = 1.5836 US dollars

Wii launched

Years 2003-2008

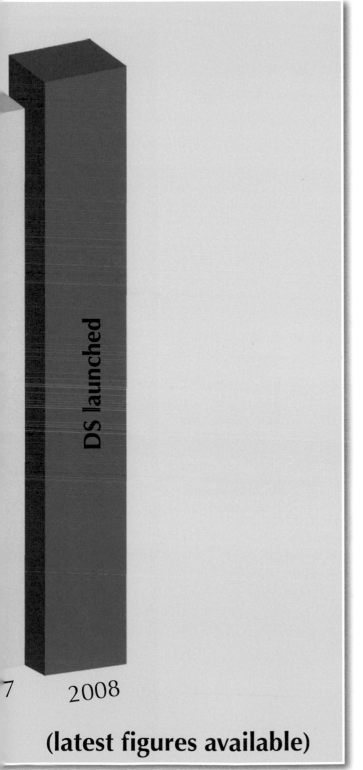

DS launched

7   2008

(latest figures available)

In 2010, Nintendo's profits fell for the first time in six years. New title production is slowing down, and the DS and Wii are both in need of updates. What are Nintendo's plans for the future?

Nintendo has recently been hit by a triple blow. Developers are producing fewer and fewer games for the Wii and DS; gamers are spending less money on high-priced titles; and both consoles need an update to stay ahead of the competition. The success of Apple's iPhone has bitten into Nintendo's market of casual gamers, while Xbox and PlayStation 3 have both launched their own versions of the Wii's groundbreaking sensor controls. What Nintendo does next will have a major effect on the company's finances for many years to come.

Thankfully for the company, two big products are on the horizon. First, a 3D version of the DS — known as the 3DS — has just launched, and is expected to give console sales a major boost, as well as breathe new life into their most famous game franchises Mario, Zelda, and Pokémon.

Satoru Iwata introduces the 3DS in 2010. The handheld console allows games to play in 3D, as well as take 3D pictures and record 3D movies.

Second, Wii HD, a new version of the best-selling console, is scheduled to hit the market in 2011. Complete with HD graphics and a bigger memory, industry insiders say the Wii HD will be a major step forward.

Nintendo doesn't intend to stop there. The company that moved from playing cards to toys and electronic games remains committed to finding and developing the next big thing to get the world playing! They have just invested almost $150 million to build new R&D headquarters in Kyoto. Nintendo's R&D division is already the envy of every other gaming company, and it looks set to improve. Watch out to see if Nintendo can change the face of gaming all over again in the next decade!

To create a new product, it is helpful to put together a product development brief like the one below. This is a sample brief for Hand-held Fitness. SWOT analysis on the page opposite can help you to think about the strengths, weaknesses, opportunities, and threats of your product. This can let you see how feasible and practical your idea is before investing in it.

Product Development Brief

Name of product: Hand-held Fitness

Type of product: Like the Wii Fit but for the DS.

The product explained (use 25 words or less): Fitness in the palm of your hand! Jogging, yoga, aerobics. Reach peak fitness with your hand-held fitness trainer!

Target age of users: 25-75

What does the product do?: The program takes the user through a series of fitness programs — from beginner to expert — using the principle of the Wii's sensor control. Put it in your pocket when you jog on the spot, or keep it in your hand when you stretch to reach that tricky yoga position. You'll never need to go to the gym again!

Are there any similar products already available?: None that I know of.

What makes your product different?: This product is innovative, easy to use, and so convenient. It's like carrying a personal trainer around in your pocket!

Name of Nintendo game you are assessing … *Hand-held Fitness*
The table below will help you assess your Nintendo game. By addressing all four areas, you can make your game stronger and more likely to be a success.

Questions to consider

Does your game do something unique?

Does it have any additional uses?

What are its USPs (unique selling points)?

Why will people use this game instead of a similar one?

Strengths

Hand-held Fitness is a world first! No other game does what we can do.

Everyone who owns a DS can use it — there is a huge potential market.

Can be used to get fit in a variety of ways — jogging, yoga, aerobics, etc. — so will appeal to different types of people who like different fitness methods.

Why wouldn't people play this game?

Does it do everything that it says it can?

Does it work on any other handheld consoles, or just the DS?

Is it better than similar games available?

Weaknesses

People who aren't interested in fitness won't play it.

The Wii Fit has been very popular, so owners of that might not want to switch.

It's a Nintendo-only game, so PSP users would have to buy a DS first.

Will the issue that the game tackles become more important over time?

Can the game be improved in the future?

Can it be used globally?

Can it develop new USPs?

Opportunities

We have first-mover advantage, and Nintendo behind us. Everyone in the world will learn about the game quickly.

Health and fitness will always be important; perhaps the government will support it?

Is the gaming market shrinking?

Is the DS facing competition from other handheld consoles?

Are any of your weaknesses so bad that they might affect the game in the long run?

Threats

There is a danger of people dropping their DS while they are exercising, and holding Nintendo responsible for the breakage.

If people suffer injuries like bad backs or strained muscles, they might also blame Nintendo.

Do You Have What It takes to Work at Nintendo?

1) How often do you play video games?
a) Rarely. I don't have a console, but I sometimes play at friends' houses.
b) A couple of times per week. We have a Wii at home, and I like ten-pin bowling.
c) Regularly. I always beat my friends, and I like to keep up to date with new releases.

2) Are you good with computers?
a) I can switch it on, but don't ask me if the printer's not working!
b) I'm alright. I hooked up our wireless router and I can restore the Internet connection if it fails.
c) I'm a whiz! I've bought books on programming, and I'm teaching myself to code.

3) Describe your perfect weekend:
a) No homework, a movie with my friends, then TV.
b) Sports in the morning, then computer games in the afternoon.
c) Couple of hours' networked gaming, then some C++ programming. Need to keep practicing!

4) It's shop class at school. Do you:
a) Put the final coat of paint on your birdhouse. It's taken three months, but it's nearly finished.
b) Make sketches of a new skyscraper you plan to build with lollipop sticks.
c) Finish your plans for a new universal remote control that also dims the lights.

5) Ever thought about designing your own video game?
a) No way. I wouldn't even know where to start.
b) I like finding the "cheats" online, but I can't imagine ever building a whole game.
c) All the time! I have three games planned out already!

6) Your hero is:
a) Tom Brady or Troy Polamalu.
b) Mark Zuckerberg — he's a young guy who created a cool new company with Facebook.
c) Shigeru Miyamoto — the undisputed king of video games who invented Mario!

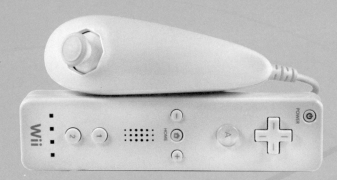

Results

Mostly As: Sorry, but your chance of working at Nintendo is looking shaky! It doesn't sound like you have the interest in computers or gaming to succeed at this cutting-edge company.

Mostly Bs: You are interested in gaming and technology, but you need to work on standing out from the pack if you want to succeed in a very competitive business.

Mostly Cs: It sounds like you have what it takes to get a job at Nintendo! Keep working hard at school and pushing to be the best, and who knows?

boom A period of rapid economic growth.

brainchild An idea or invention.

charismatic Describes individuals possessing certain qualities or powers that allow them to influence and inspire large numbers of people.

components Working parts of a device.

consumer A person who purchases goods or services for his or her own personal needs.

corporate philosophy The beliefs or goals of a company.

distribution Delivery of products across a large area.

dominance Control over something, e.g. the games market.

entrepreneur A person who organizes and manages a business, usually with considerable initiative and risk.

evolution Gradual development into a more complicated or advanced form.

high-tech/low-tech product A seemingly complicated and sophisticated product that works on a very simple principle.

import To buy or bring in goods from a foreign country.

indispensable Essential; absolutely necessary.

ingenious Skillful or clever.

innovation Something newly introduced, like a new piece of technology or a new way of doing something.

intellectual property Ideas or inventions, like the Wii's motion sensor, that are 'owned' by their creator and can be legally protected.

legalize To make something legal, or allowed by law.

Meccano A construction set consisting of small metal and plastic parts, which could be made into mechanical models.

patent A government grant to an inventor, giving him or her the right to be the only person to make, use, and sell the invention for a limited period of time.

physiotherapy The treatment of an illness or injury through exercise and massage.

recoding Reprogramming; rewriting the code that makes a game work.

rehabilitate To help someone return to health, or return to a former condition.

retailer A company that sells goods in small quantities to consumers.

revenue A company's income before costs are taken into account; gross income.

stock price The value of company shares at a specific time.

subsidiary A company with at least 50 percent of its stock owned by another company.

tax A financial contribution imposed by a government on a country's citizens to raise money.

USP (Unique Selling Proposition or Point) A unique quality about a company's product or service that will attract customers to use or buy it rather than an alternative product.

wireless network A collection of computers that are not connected by cables, but can still share and transfer information.

withstand To resist or be able to cope with.

Academy of Interactive Arts & Sciences (AIAS)
23622 Calabasas Road, Suite 300
Calabasas, CA 91302
(818) 876-0826
Web site: http://www.interactive.org

The mission of the AIAS is to promote and advance the worldwide interactive entertainment community; recognize outstanding achievements in the interactive arts and sciences; and host an annual awards show, the Interactive Achievement Awards, to enhance awareness of the interactive art form.

Educational Computing Organization of Ontario (ECOO)
10 Morrow Avenue, Suite 202
Toronto, ON M6R 2J1
Canada
(416) 489-1713
Web site: http://www.ecoo.org

ECOO helps teachers and students in coordinating computer learning into the educational process.

Entertainment Software Association (ESA)
575 7th Street NW
Suite 300
Washington, DC 20004
Web site: http://www.theesa.com

The Entertainment Software Association (ESA) is the US association exclusively dedicated to serving the business and public affairs needs of companies that publish computer and video games for video game consoles, personal computers, and the Internet. The ESA offers a range of services to interactive entertainment software publishers including a global anti-piracy program, business and consumer research, government relations, and intellectual property protection efforts. The ESA also owns and operates the E3 Expo.

Entertainment Software Rating Board (ESRB)
317 Madison Avenue, 22nd Floor
New York, NY 10017
Web site: http://www.esrb.org/index-js.jsp

The ESRB is a non-profit, self-regulatory body established in 1994 by the Entertainment Software Association (ESA). The ESRB assigns computer and video game content ratings, enforces industry-adopted advertising guidelines and helps ensure responsible online privacy practices for the interactive entertainment software industry.

International Game Developers Association (IGDA)
19 Mantua Road
Mt. Royal, NJ 08061
(856)-423-2990
Web site: http://www.igda.org

The International Game Developers Association is the largest non-profit membership organization serving individuals who create video games. It brings together developers at conferences, in local chapters, and in special interest groups to improve their lives and craft.

Media Awareness Network
1500 Merivale Road, 3rd Floor
Ottawa, ON K2E6Z5
Canada

(613) 224-7721

Web site: http://www.media-awareness.ca

The Media Awareness Network is a Canadian nonprofit organization that has been pioneering the development of media literacy and digital literacy programs since its incorporation in 1996. MNet's Web site offers media literacy and digital literacy materials on a wide range of media, including Internet, television, film, video games, newspapers, advertising, and popular music.

Web sites

Due to the changing nature of Internet links, Rosen Publishing has developed an online list of Web sites related to the subject of this book. This site is updated regularly. Please use this link to access this list:

http://www.rosenlinks.com/bht/nin

Ashcraft, Brian, and Jean Snow. *Arcade Mania: The Turbo-Charged World of Japan's Game Centers*. New York, NY: Kodansha, 2009.

Bissell, Tom. Extra Lives: *Why Video Games Matter*. New York, NY: Pantheon Books, 2010.

Clark, Neils, and Scott P. Shavaun. *Game Addiction: The Experience and the Effects*. Jefferson, NC: McFarland, 2009.

Dini, Kourosh. *Video Game Play and Addiction*. Bloomington, IN: iUniverse, 2008.

Donovan, Tristan. *Replay: The History of Video Games*. East Sussex, England: Yellow Ant, 2010.

Firestone, Mary. *Nintendo: The Company and Its Founders*. Edina, MN: Essential Library, 2011.

Inoue, Osamu. *Nintendo Magic: Winning the Videogame Wars*. New York, NY: Vertical, 2010.

Jenisch, Josh. *The Art of the Video Game*. Philadelphia, PA: Quirk Books, 2008.

Loguidice, Bill, and Matt Barton. *Vintage Games: An Insider Look at the History of Grand Theft Auto, Super Mario, and the Most Influential Games of All Time*. Burlington, MA: Focal Press, 2009.

Maltman, Thomas James. *The Electrifying, Action-Packed, Unusual History of Video Games*. Mankato, MN: Capstone Press, 2010.

Nagle, Jeanne. *Frequently Asked Questions about Wii and Video Game Injuries and Fitness*. New York, NY: Rosen Publishing, 2009.

Perkins, Todd. *Nintendo Wii Flash Game Creator's Guide: Design, Develop, and Share Your Games Online*. New York, NY: McGraw-Hill, 2008.

Ryan, Jeff. *Super Mario: How Nintendo Conquered America*. Portfolio, 2011.

Sloan, Daniel. *Playing to Wiin: Nintendo and the Video Game Industry's Greatest Comeback*. Hoboken, NJ: John Wiley & Sons, 2011.

Wolf, Mark, J.P. *The Video Game Explosion: A History from PONG to PlayStation and Beyond*. Westport, CT: Greenwood, 2007.

advertising   31

Donkey Kong   4, 30, 31

EAD   24, 25

Game & Watch   15, 16, 18

Game Boy   4, 15, 18, 19, 20, 22, 28

GameCube   4, 21, 26, 33

Iwata, Satoru   5, 15, 21, 26, 28, 33, 37

Mario   4, 26, 30, 31, 39

Miyamoto, Shigeru   25, 28, 30, 31

Murai, Kichibei   8

Nintendo   64, 4, 21, 22

Nintendo DS   4, 22, 26, 28–29, 36, 39

Nintendo Entertainment System (NES)   4, 15, 18, 21, 33

Nintendo Koppai   6–7, 8

playing cards   6–7, 8, 11

PlayStation   21, 22, 26, 35, 39

Pokémon   4, 19, 26, 39

public relations   28

Ray Gun SP   15, 26

research and development   18

Sony   20, 21, 22, 26, 35

Takeda, Genyo   33

Tezuka, Takashi   25

Uemura, Masayuki   18

Ultra Hand   12, 15

Wii   4, 22, 26, 32, 33, 35, 36–37, 39, 40

Xbox   35, 39

Yamauchi, Fusajiro   6–8

Yamauchi, Hiroshi   8, 10–12, 15, 16, 26, 28

Yamauchi, Sekiryo Kaneda   8

Yokoi, Gunpei   14–15, 16, 19

Zelda   4, 26, 31, 39